TARGET
Comprehension ③

SKILLS
- **Vocabulary**
- **Reasoning**
- **Planning**
- **Summarising**
- **Word recognition**
- **Writing ability**

Compiled and Edited by: Manpreet Kaur Aden

Illustrated by: Suman S. Roy

Designed by: Rakesh Kumar

Graded • Illustrations & Images • Variety of Genres

All rights are reserved. No part of this book may be reproduced, stored in a retrieval system or transmitted, in any form or by any means, mechanical, photocopying, recording or otherwise, without any prior written permission of the publisher.

1st Impression

© B. Jain Publishers (P) Ltd.

Published by
Kuldeep Jain
for
Pegasus
An imprint of
B. Jain Publishers (P) Ltd.
An ISO 9001 : 2000 Certified Company
1921, Street No. 10, Chuna Mandi, Paharganj, New Delhi-110055 (INDIA)
Tel: 91-11-4567 1000 | Fax: 91-11-4567 1010
Website: **www.bjain.com** | E-mail: **info@bjain.com**

ISBN: 978-81-319-3227-8

Printed in India : JJ Imprints Pvt. Ltd. Noida.

Objectives of Comprehension

It is often seen that whenever children are made to do a comprehension exercise, seldom are they made aware of the purpose of the whole exercise. Many a time, even the guardian or the teacher is not clear about the purpose. Of course, we are all well informed about the common purpose like comprehension teaches a child to maintain his attention and also that it teaches them to use strategies to enhance understanding of the reading material. Given below are some of the common objectives of comprehension:

- *Getting to understand the main idea of the text*
- *Noting the correct sequence of the text*
- *Recognizing the key words of the text*
- *Making reasonable and logical conclusion after reading the text*
- *Recognizing the different genres of the text*
- *Identifying fiction from non-fiction*
- *Distinguishing fantasy from realism*
- *Recognizing the theme, plot and characters of the given passage*

What it is to monitor one's own comprehension?

Children should be trained from a very early age of how to monitor their own comprehension. Sometimes text does not make sense as one reads it and students need to learn to recognize when this happens. At once they should stop to fix it. Students should stop regularly and check while reading to make sure that they understand what they are reading. Reread and think again and again. They should read to the end of the page, think, and see if they are still confused. Learn the strategy of decoding multi-syllabic words. The students should be able to summarize a variety of written texts.

This series **Target Comprehension** is an excellently planned and graded series which brings together a diverse range of passages for the children to read. All the reading material that occurs in this book are judged on the basis of theme, language and the overall readability of the passages. The activities are graded too and fit in justly with the passages.

Contents

1. Masha and the Bear 6
2. The Monkey's Heart 12
3. Gathering Leaves 19
4. Email 24
5. The Quest of Cleverness 29
6. Volcano 35
7. The Meeting of Robin Hood and Little John 41
8. Giraffe 48
9. The Elves and the Shoemaker 53
10. Helicopter 59
11. Friends Abbie Farwell Brown 65
12. J.K. Rowling 70
13. King Midas' Touch 74
14. The Wolf and the Seven Young Kids 79
15. Halloween 86
16. The Fieldmouse 93
17. Victoria Falls 97
18. Sindbad the Sailor 102

Fun to Know

A warming up discussion

Have you ever been anywhere with your friends?

Have you ever played a trick on anyone?

Masha and the Bear

Once upon a time there lived an old man with his wife. They had a pretty little granddaughter named Masha. One day some friends of Masha decided to go to the forest to gather mushrooms and berries. Masha too wanted to go with her friends. So she asked her grandparents for their permission.

'You may go but keep close to the others and do not get lost,' her grandparents warned her.

Soon, Masha and her friends were in the forest looking for mushrooms and berries. And before she knew it, she had left her friends far behind! When at last she saw that she was all alone, she began to call her friends loudly.

'O dear! I am lost. What shall I do now?' she thought worried.

But without wasting anymore time, Masha started walking. Soon, she saw a little cottage. Masha knocked on the door.

'Is anybody there?' she called out.

But there was no answer. So she gave the door a push and the door opened! Masha went inside and sat down on a bench to rest.

Now in that cottage lived a great big Bear. He had gone out for his morning walk. Soon, the Bear returned. He was very pleased to see Masha.

'Aha, it's really nice of you to come to my house young lady! Now I'll never let you go! You will live in my house, cook my food and be my faithful servant,' said the Bear. Masha could do nothing to escape. So she stayed with the Bear and worked for him.

Every morning, the Bear would go to the forest for the day. Before leaving he would tell Masha, 'You must never go out without me, for if you do, I will catch you and eat you up!'

So Masha sat thinking how she could get away from the terrible Bear. The cottage was surrounded on all sides by the forest and she did not know the way out. She thought and thought until she knew what to do.

That day, when the Bear came back from the forest, Masha said, 'Bear, please let me go to my village for a day. I want to take pies for my Grandma and Grandpa.'

'No, I cannot allow you to go through the forest. You will get lost,' said the Bear. 'But if you like I can take the pies to your Grandma and Grandpa.'

Now that was exactly what Masha wanted to hear! She baked some pies, put them on a plate and took out a very large basket. Then she told the

Bear, 'I'll put the pies in the basket. But remember, you are not to open the basket on the way and eat the pies! I am going to climb to the top of the big oak tree and will see you all the time.'

'Very well,' said the Bear and went outside to see if it was raining. Masha quickly crawled into the basket and covered herself with the plate of pies. When the Bear came in, he saw the basket, strapped it on his back and started off. Tramp-tramp went the Bear amidst the spruce trees up the hill and down the valley.

After a long walk, the Bear was tired and sat down to rest.

'If I don't rest my bones, I think I will die. Perhaps, I can also eat a pie,' said the Bear to himself.

At once, Masha called out from the basket, 'I CAN SEE YOU! Don't sit on the stump and don't eat my pie! Take it to my Grandma and Grandpa.

'Dear me! What sharp eyes Masha has,' thought the Bear. 'She sees everything!'

So, the Bear picked up the basket and went on. Soon, he stopped again and said, 'If I don't rest my bones, I think I will die! So I'll sit under a tree and eat a pie.'

But Masha called out again from the basket, 'I CAN SEE YOU! Don't sit under the tree and don't eat my pie! Take it to my Grandma and Grandpa!'

'What a clever little girl Masha is,' said the Bear. 'Though she is sitting high up on a tree and is far away, she sees all I do and she hears all I say!'

Again, the Bear got to his feet and started walking faster than before. Soon he reached the village where Masha lived. Without any difficulty he found Masha's grandparents house. The Bear started banging on the door loudly.

'Open the gate,' cried the Bear. 'I have brought something for you from Masha!'

But before Masha's grandparents could let him in, the villagers rushed out at him, shouting. Frightened, the Bear set down the basket by the door and ran away as fast as he could. Hearing so much noise, Masha's grandparents opened the door and saw the basket.

'What is in the basket dear?' the old woman asked.

The old man lifted the lid and looked inside. He could not believe his eyes. For there in the basket sat Masha alive and well! The old man and woman were overjoyed. They were happy to be together again. And from then on, Masha never went to the forest again.

 **Let's remember the story**

1. Why did Masha want to go to the forest?
2. What did her grandparents tell her?
3. What did the Bear ask Masha to do?
4. How did Masha trick the Bear?
5. What did Masha do when the Bear thought of eating a pie?
6. What happened when the Bear reached the village?

Practice writing sentences

Read the words given below and make sentences using them.

1. Permission

   ....

   ....

2. Cottage

   ....

   ....

3. Escape

   ....

   ....

4. Large

   ....

   ....

5. Loudly

   ....

   ....

6. Basket

   ....

   ....

Prefix and suffix

Given below are a few **prefix** and **suffix** along with a number of words. Use them together to make new words.

un-	re-	-ness	-ly
happy equal	do mother	act light	appear kind
wild mask			sad kept

....

....

....

....

Find friends

You are familiar with similar sounding words called **rhyming words**. Read the words in Column A aloud and write a similar sounding word in front of them in Column B.

Column A	Column B
Lost	
Walk	
Bake	
Hill	
Fast	
Found	

11

Fun to Know

A warming up discussion

Have you ever seen an island?
What do you know about crocodiles?

The Monkey's Heart

It was a long time ago when this story took place. In a deep forest, there lived a wise monkey. He was so intelligent that his fame spread all across the forests. All the animals greatly admired him. Now, this monkey had his home on a tree on the shore of a wide river. Each day, he used to go to an island in the middle of the river to eat delicious fruits which grew there.

He used to jump on the big rock that was between the river shore and the island to reach the island. Now, a crocodile and his wife lived in the river. Each day, the crocodile's wife used to see the monkey as he went back and forth between the island and the river shore. It was then that a longing developed in her heart. She thought about her longing all the time and soon looked weaker.

Her husband, the crocodile was troubled. One day, he asked her, 'What is troubling you, my dear? You look weaker as each day goes by.'

So at last, she told her husband, 'I want to eat the heart of the wise monkey that goes to the island each day. Everyday, he eats the delicious fruits that grow there. I have sometimes eaten the delicious fruits which fall into the river. How delicious would his heart be after eating such delicacies each day?'

'Good wife,' said the crocodile, 'I live in the water and he lives on dry land. How can I catch him?'

'He must be caught. If I don't get him, I shall die,' said his wife. 'You must find a way.'

'All right,' said the crocodile, 'I will think of something to get you the monkey's heart.'

The next day, while the monkey was returning from the island, he saw that the rock over which he jumped was bigger than on other days. He became suspicious. But then, he thought something and jumped on the rock. The next moment, the crocodile began moving. But the monkey was not afraid.

'Who are you and where are you taking me?' demanded the monkey.

Hearing this, the crocodile said, 'I live in this river with my wife. Each day, I saw you when you jumped. I wanted to meet you, so I sat on the rock.'

'Sir Crocodile,' the monkey answered. 'Why is it that you wanted to meet me?'

'Well actually, I wanted to take you to my home as my wife wants to meet you,' said the crocodile. 'If you will be so kind as to come with me, I shall be grateful to you.'

The monkey thought and said, 'I shall go with you. But I wonder why your wife wants to meet me.'

The crocodile thought about these words and decided that it would be better to tell the truth to the monkey before he took him home. He also realized that the monkey was trapped. As the monkey was unable to swim, he would not be going anywhere.

So, the crocodile said, 'You think I am carrying you to meet my wife out of pure good nature? Not at all! My wife wants to eat your heart. Today, I have caught you in a trap and you cannot escape.'

'Friend,' said the monkey, 'I am so glad that you have told me the truth. Well, Sir Crocodile, we monkeys jump from tree to tree. Don't you think that if we kept our hearts with us, it would be all knocked to pieces!'

The crocodile was surprised to hear this. 'Well, where do you keep your heart then?' asked the crocodile.

The wise monkey pointed towards a fig tree on the shore with clusters of ripe fruit on it. 'See,' said he, 'there are our hearts hanging on that fig tree. If you will allow me to go I shall bring my heart for your wife to eat.'

'If that is so,' said the crocodile, 'then I won't have to kill you.'

And without another thought, the crocodile brought the monkey on the shore of the river. At once, the monkey leapt off the crocodile's back, ran towards the fig tree and climbed it.

'Quickly, give me your heart,' cried out the crocodile.

'Oh silly crocodile!' said the monkey. 'Have you ever heard of any creature that keeps its heart out of its body! I had said so to save myself. Now, that I know that your wife wants to kill me, I shall no longer go to the island to eat the fruits there. Be gone, for though you have a large body but you have no brain.'

The crocodile was disappointed for he had been fooled by the wise monkey. He slowly turned around and sadly went towards his home.

Let's remember the story

1. Why was the monkey famous?
2. Where did the monkey go to eat fruits?
3. Why did the crocodile's wife want to eat the monkey's heart?
4. Why did the crocodile speak the truth?
5. What did the monkey do after hearing this?
6. What did the monkey tell the crocodile in the end?

Circling the words

Read the passage given below. Circle all the **doing words** or **verbs** in the passage.

Butterflies are small, beautiful insects. You must have seen them hovering

over or sitting on flowers. Did you know that there are seventeen thousand different kinds of butterflies on Earth! Butterflies have different shapes and sizes.

Butterflies have to go through four main stages of life. The first stage is the egg stage followed by the larva stage. The larva eats as much as possible. As it grows, it sheds it outer skin. After a few weeks, the caterpillar goes into the chrysalis stage. In this stage, the larva slowly and gradually becomes a butterfly.

When the butterfly comes out from the chrysalis, it pumps blood to its wings so that it can fly. And then the butterfly flies to the flowers to suck their nectar.

Practice writing sentences

Read the words given below and make sentences using them.

1. River

   ....

2. Wise

   ....

3. Weaker

   ....

4. Afraid

   ....

5. Trap

   ....

6. Climb

   ....

 **Antonyms**

Read the words given below in two columns. Can you match the words that have the opposite meaning?

Words	Antonyms
Afraid	Below
First	Fast
Above	Brave
Truth	Backward
Slow	Last
Forward	Lie

 **Explore new places**

You must be knowing what an island is. With the help of your teacher, get to know about an island which is large enough to be a continent. Explore Australia.

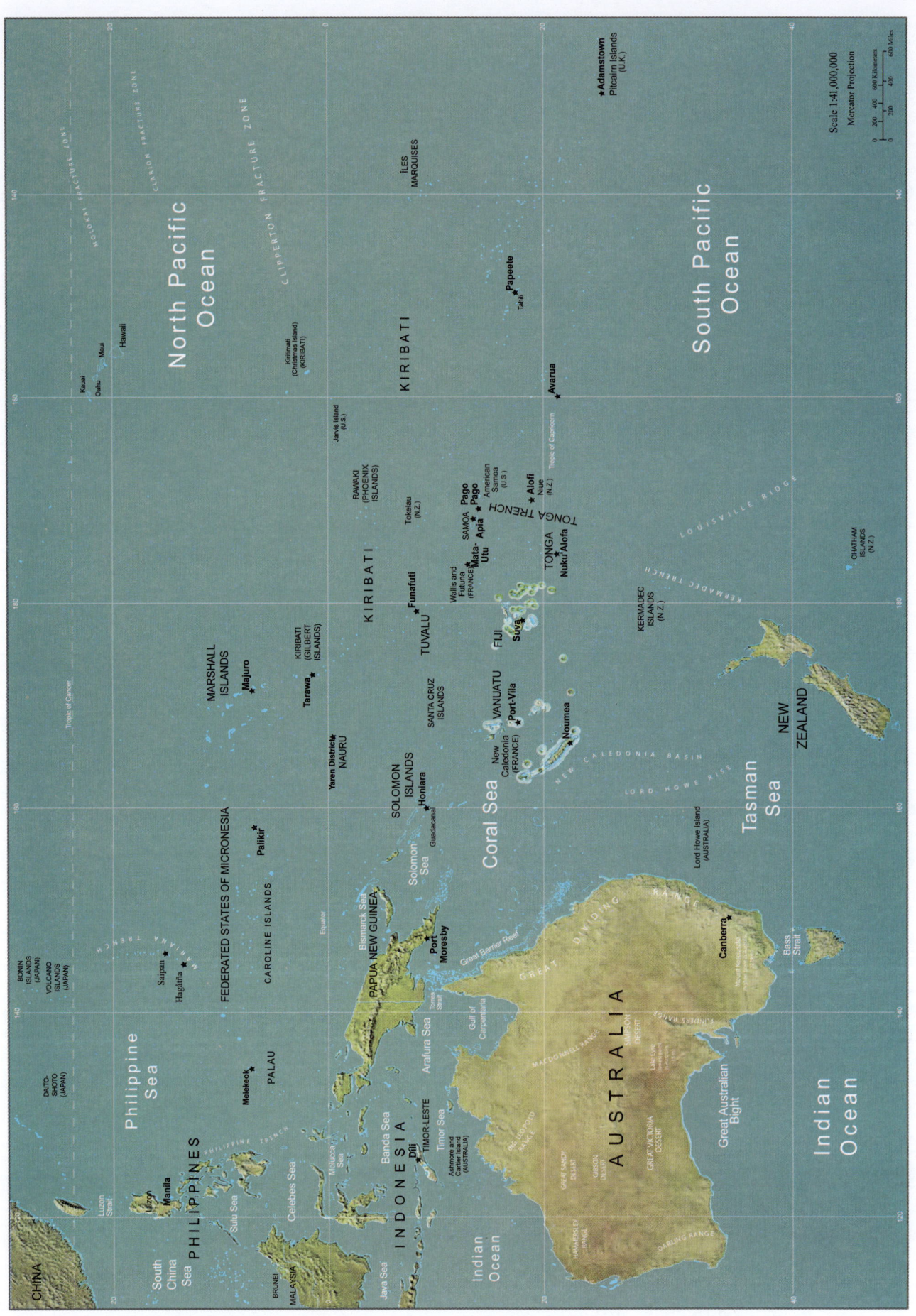

Fun to Know

3

A warming up discussion

Do you like Autumn?
Why do the trees shed leaves?

Gathering Leaves
By Robert Frost

Spades take up leaves

No better than spoons,

And bags full of leaves

Are light as balloons.

I make a great noise

Of rustling all day

Like rabbit and deer

Running away.

But the mountains I raise

Elude my embrace,

Flowing over my arms

And into my face.

I may load and unload

Again and again

Till I fill the whole shed,

And what have I then?

Next to nothing for weight,
And since they grew duller
From contact with earth,
Next to nothing for color.

Next to nothing for use.
But a crop is a crop,
And who's to say where
The harvest shall stop?

 **Let's remember the story**

1. Why were the bags full of leaves light as balloons?
2. Who is the narrator of the poem?
3. With whom do the leaves compare themselves?
4. How are the leaves useful in raising a crop?
5. Where are the leaves kept once they are collected?

 **Complete the sentences**

Read the sentences given below and complete them with the help of the poem.

1. The mountains I.. embrace.
2. I may load... again.
3. ....leaves... spoons.
4. ....arms .... face.
5. From contact... nothing for................
6. I make.. all day.

Idioms

A group of words which have a different meaning compared to the written/spoken words are **idioms**. Match the idioms given in Column A with their meanings in Column B.

Idioms	Meanings
Around the clock	Very lazy
Behind the times	Sensible
A couch potato	Very easy
Down to earth	Short sleep or nap
Easy as pie	All the time
Forty winks	Old fashioned

Would you tell us about your favourite season? Why do you like it?

....

....

....

....

....

....

....
....
....
....
....
....
....
....

Fun to Know

A warming up discussion
Do you use a computer?
Did you ever leave a message for someone on the computer?

Email

Have you ever sent an email or perhaps seen your parents do so? Watching them, have you ever thought how emails came to be? Email also known as electronic mail was thought of only some time back. When computer had become popular, people in work places used to leave a small message for the others to read when they turned on the computer. It was like a note on someone's desk or a note attached to a magnet on the refrigerator. Things were that simple back then.

Probably the first email system that could send messages to another person working on the same computer was MAILBOX. It was used in 1965.

But this system gave way to SNDMSG, another early program to send messages on the same computer but to its different users.

During that time, computers were not everywhere. So, one computer was used by many users. In this case, the users left messages for others to read on the same computer. But with time, as more people became computers users and computers became connected to each other over the network, the situation became complex.

It now became necessary that the message which was left on the computer for others to read should now be left for specific people.

To put it simply, the message left on the computer now needed to have an address and an envelope to keep it inside. It would mean that only to whom the message was written would be able to see it and read it and send a reply back. To do this, it was necessary that the users have addresses. It would be then easy to send the message with an address to only specific people.

It was then that Ray Tomlinson invented email. He did so in 1972. Like many of the Internet inventors, Tomlinson also worked for Bolt Beranek and Newman as an ARPANET contractor. He was working on SNDMSG a 'local' electronic message program. Using this program one could leave a message for others who worked on that same computer. Tomlinson used a file transfer protocol that he was working on called CYPNET to adapt the SNDMSG program. By doing so he could send electronic messages to any computer on the ARPANET network. He used the @ symbol from a computer keyboard to indicate those messages that were sent from one computer to the other over the network. Now, anyone using the internet had but to type the name of the user @ the name of the computer. In no time this method of sending messages became popular.

The first email was sent between two computers that were kept side by side. The email was sent using the ARPANET network.

The World Wide Web offers a lot to do but sending an email remains the most popular application of the internet. With time, as this means to send messages became popular, it was made more users friendly. Larry Roberts invented some email folders to sort the mail that his boss received. It became a defining feature of email. In 1975 John Vital developed some software to organize email. By 1976 email had really taken off, and commercial packages began to appear. Within a couple of years, 75% of all ARPANET traffic was email.

Initially what began as a luxury for a few is not used the world over. Today, more than 600 million people use email internationally.

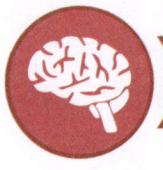

Let's remember the story

1. How did people first left messages for others on the computer?
2. One computer was used by many people. Why?
3. What could make the message reach only a particular person?
4. Who invented the email? What sign did he use from his keyboard?
5. Where was the first email sent?
6. What became the defining feature of the email?

Practice writing sentences

Read the words given below and make sentences using them.

1. Message

   ....

2. Magnet

   ....

3. Popular

   ....

4. Appear

   ....

5. Side

   ....

6. More

   ....

Synonyms

Read the words given below in two columns. Can you match the words that have the **same** meaning?

Words	Synonyms
Cunning	Wide
Quick	Empty
Broad	Untrue
Loyal	Clever
False	Faithful
Vacant	Fast

g) Circling the words

Read the passage given below and circle all the **describing words** or **adjectives**.

The magnificent Redwood Trees are some of the largest trees in the world! They are found mostly in northern California where cool temperatures, misty rains, and dense fog allow them to grow. However, these giants can also grow in other areas but they may not grow to their giant size.

Redwood Trees can live for many thousands of years. These old trees can grow up to be more than 370 feet tall! That would make these trees taller than the Statue of Liberty! A few among these giants are so wide that roads can be built through them. Redwoods Trees are preserved in California's Redwood National Park.

Fun to Know

A warming up discussion

What do you mean by the word quest?
Do you know what giants are?

The Quest of Cleverness

Long ago, a distant kingdom was ruled by an intelligent king. However, the king had a foolish son. The king sent his son to school hoping that learning new things would put an end to his son's foolishness. But in no time, the teachers gave up on the prince. They said, 'It is no use teaching this boy through books. It is a waste of our valuable time.'

Then, the king called his wise counsel. 'How can I make the prince wise and clever?' the king asked them. The counsel discussed the matter over for many days. At last, they said, 'Your Majesty, send the prince on a journey. In this manner he might learn things which his teachers have been unable to teach him through books.'

The king liked this suggestion. So, a splendid black horse was prepared for the prince's journey. He was also given fine weapons and a big bag full of money. The king blessed his son as he was ready to depart.

The prince journeyed through many lands. He learnt something new from each country that he passed through. He met all kinds of people, old and young, rich and poor and acquired knowledge. And so, the prince who could not understand anything written in books learned many things during his journey.

Then, the prince arrived in a city where an auction was going on. The prince too went to the auction. There he saw a songbird being offered for sale. 'What is the specialty of this songbird?' asked the prince. 'This bird, on its owner's command, can sing a song which will put anyone to sleep,' came the reply.

The prince thought that the bird was worth purchasing and bought the bird. Next, he saw a beetle offered for sale. He learnt that the beetle could

gnaw its way through any wall in the world. So, he bought the beetle too. Next, he bought a butterfly that could carry any amount of weight on its strong wings.'

When the auction was over, the prince once again resumed his wanderings with these priced possessions. Soon, he reached a vast forest where before he knew it he had lost his way. As the foliage in the forest was thick, the prince climbed the tallest tree to see the way out of the forest.

Sitting on the highest branch, the prince saw a mountain at a distance. He quickly got down and went towards the mountain. But once there, he saw that it wasn't a mountain at all! It was a wall which surrounded the land of the giants! Then, the prince saw a giant standing on the wall. But before the giant could see him, the prince commanded its songbird to sing and the giant was soon fast sleep.

The prince then asked the beetle to gnaw at the wall surrounding the land of the giants. Soon, the beetle had gnawed an entrance through the wall, big enough for the prince to go inside. No sooner had the prince taken a step inside that he found himself in a dungeon. And to his surprise a beautiful princess stood before him. You see, the beetle had gnawed at the wall where the dungeons were located in the land of the giants.

The prince learnt that the princess was a captive of the giants. One of the many things that the prince had learned during his wanderings was that 'Always rescue a fair maiden in distress.' Wasting no time, the prince asked the princess, 'How can I rescue you, princess?' 'You will never succeed in rescuing me,' she said.

'A giant guards the entrance to this land,' added the princess. 'No one can go past him.' 'That is no trouble at all,' said the prince. 'I will take care

of him.' Just at that moment, a giant entered the dungeon hearing their voices.

'Sing, my little bird,' the prince commanded his songbird. No sooner had the bird burst into a melody that the giant fell on the floor and started snoring.

'But how will we climb the high wall surrounding this land,' inquired the princess. 'We don't need to climb the wall,' said the prince. 'My beetle has already made a way in the wall. And the guard standing on the wall has already been put to sleep. Now, let us go.'

Quickly, the prince and princess went out of the land of the giants. As the princess was exhausted from her captivity, she sat on the butterfly's wings which at once started flying.

Then, with the princess sitting on the butterfly's wings, the prince led them out of the forest. Once out of the forest, the prince went towards his father's kingdom with the princess beside him. It was sometime before the prince reached his father's kingdom. The king was overjoyed to see his son and welcomed him with open arms. The prince told the king about all of his adventures and showed him the songbird, the gnawing beetle and the strong-winged butterfly. The king and the counselors were convinced that the prince was no longer foolish. Sometime later, the prince and the princess were married and the prince after his father ruled his kingdom wisely and justly.

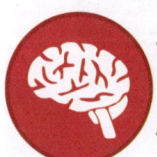

Let's remember the story

1. What did the counsel advise the king?
2. Which three things did the prince buy at the auction?
3. What was the ability of the songbird?

4. Why was the beetle special?
5. How did the prince escape the land of the giants?
6. How did the prince and princess come out of the forest?

Prefix and suffix

Given below are a few **prefix** and **suffix** along with a number of words. Use them together to make new words.

-y	-less	in-	mis-
aim   lead   air   cheer   match   mess
victor   ice   side   jump   take   age
treat   haste

....

....

....

....

....

Antonyms

Read the words given below in two columns. Can you match the words that have the **opposite** meaning?

Words	Antonyms
Alike	Fear
Freeze	Hilly
Connect	Different
Flat	Never
Courage	Melt
Always	Separate

Practice writing sentences

Read the words given below and make sentences using them.

1. Journey

   ....

2. Learn

   ....

3. Wise

   ....

4. Giant

   ....

5. Rescue

   ....

6. Bless

   ....

Fun to Know

6 **A warming up discussion**
What is a volcano?
Have you seen a volcano eruption on the ttelevision?

Volcano

A volcano is a mountain from which molten rocks, rocks and ash comes out. It has a large pool of molten rock below the earth's surface. Volcanoes are found all over the earth. But it is not always that a volcano erupts.

The eruptions in the volcanoes take place when pressure deep inside the earth's surface builds up. Gases and rock shoot up through the opening and spill over or fill the air with lava fragments. However, lava is not the only thing that comes out during the eruptions. An eruption can also cause lateral blasts, avalanches, hot ash flows and even floods and mudslides. Volcano eruptions have been known to destroy entire forests. An erupting volcano can also cause tsunamis, flash floods, earthquakes, mudflows and even rock falls.

You will wonder how volcanoes are formed. Well, our earth's crust is made up of huge pieces of rocks. You would know that these rocks move all the time. You do not feel their movement because these rocks move very, very slowly. As these plates move, sometimes small gaps remain and the extremely hot magma deep inside the earth rises up through these gaps to the earth's surface. As it rises, the earth's surface too rises up forming volcanoes. At the surface, the magma inside the volcano comes out during an eruption in the form of lava flows and ash deposits. Do you know that as the volcanoes continue to erupt, it gets bigger and bigger?

Volcanoes can be categorized as active, dormant or extinct. An active volcano is one which has erupted in recent times and there is a possibility that it may erupt again soon. A dormant volcano is one which has not erupted for a long time but there is a possibility it can erupt in the future. However, an extinct volcano is one which has not erupted for thousand of years and there is no possibility that it will erupt again in future.

Did you know that are more than 1500 active volcanoes on the Earth! Many of these volcanoes are under the sea. The volcanoes under the sea, when they erupt, they also aid in the formation of new islands. Interestingly, the area around a volcano has very many earthquakes. The Pacific Ring of Fire has the most number of volcanoes in the world. It has about 452 volcanoes, 75% of these volcanoes are either active or perhaps dormant.

According to their shape and structure, volcanoes can be divided into four types—cinder cones, composite volcanoes, shield volcanoes and lava volcanoes. Do you know that sometimes scientists find the summits of volcanoes covered with snow! They have even found deep lakes on the summits of volcanoes.

Volcanoes are forces of nature that destroy all that comes in the way of the flowing lava. But it also benefits the human beings. As the volcano erupts, its ash settles down on the ground, making the soil of that area very good for vegetation. As the lava flows, cools and settles down, it forms new lands. Volcanoes also release carbon dioxide and hydrogen that help boost the process of photosynthesis in plants and the hydrogen after mixing with oxygen becomes water vapour that adds to the water cycle.

Let's remember the story

1. What is a volcano?
2. Why do volcanoes erupt?
3. What are the three categories of volcanoes?
4. What is a dormant volcano?
5. Name a few benefits of a volcano.
6. Name a few things that are part of a volcano eruption.

Complete the sentences

Read the sentences carefully and complete them.

1. An eruption can..
2. An extinct volcano has not..

3. Hot magma rises... earth's surface.

4. Volcanoes under.................................. erupt................................... islands

5. Volcano summits..

6. Volcanoes also give out..

Fiery grid

Can you find the name of 7 volcanoes in the grid given below?

| Paricutin | Mauna Loa | Vesuvius | Fuji | Krakatoa | Tambora | Pelee |

P	F	T	A	H	I	A	A	R	M
A	E	P	K	R	A	S	P	P	A
R	V	E	S	U	V	I	U	S	U
I	E	L	O	U	N	J	O	C	N
C	F	E	T	A	M	B	O	R	A
U	U	E	A	P	E	T	A	E	L
T	J	S	E	L	N	M	R	R	O
I	I	K	R	A	K	A	T	O	A
N	I	M	C	U	T	I	A	Z	P

Find friends

You are familiar with similar sounding words called **rhyming words**. Read the words in Column A aloud and write a similar sounding word in front of them in Column B.

Column A	Column B
Rock	
Pool	
Flow	
Cone	
Boost	
Found	

Volcano Wiz Kid

Lava molten rock that comes out of a volcano

Magma molten rock inside the earth

Magma chamber large pool of molten rock inside the earth

Crater a cup shaped hole on top of a volcano

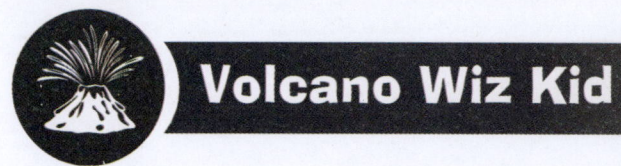

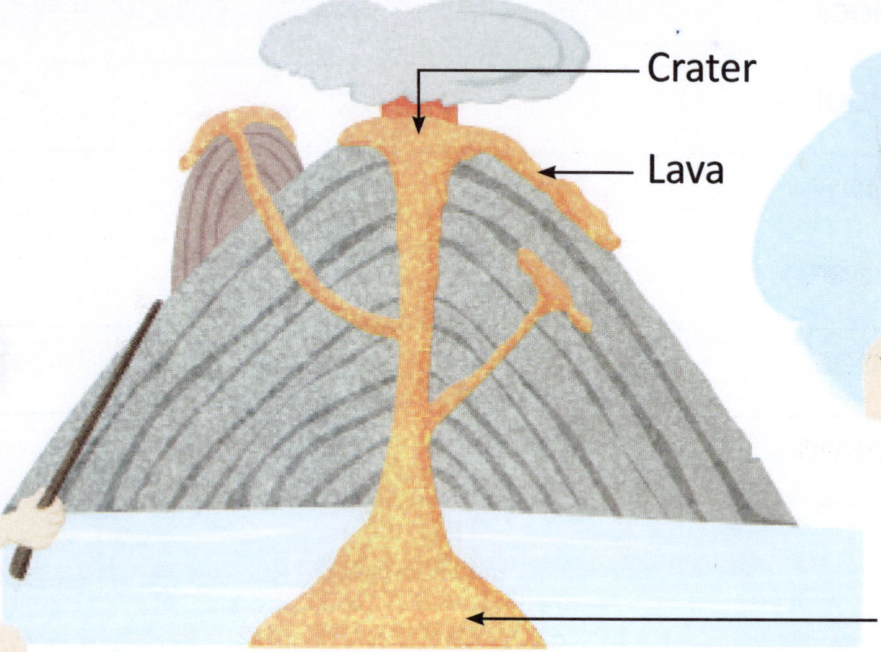

Crater

Lava

Magma chamber

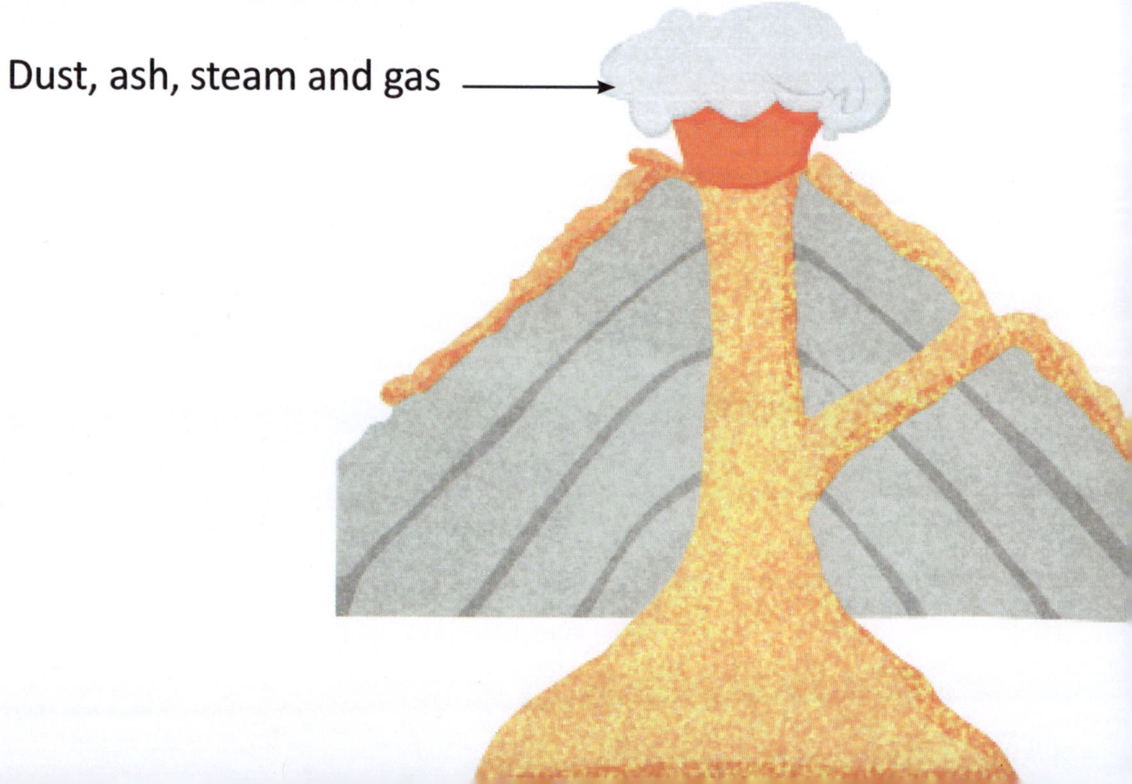

Dust, ash, steam and gas

Fun to Know

A warming up discussion

Have you ever seen a forest?
Do you know who Robin Hood was?

The Meeting of Robin Hood and Little John

This story had taken place long ago. It was the time when kings ruled and travelling to different cities took days and weeks. During this time lived Robin Hood. He was a bandit. A bandit is someone who is a robber. He lived in the Sherwood Forest in England with his men. People fondly called his men 'Merry Men'.

One day, Robin Hood was walking in the forest all by himself. He had his bow and arrows with him. Soon, he came to a river. Its water was fast flowing. A small, narrow bridge was made to cross the river. Only one person could cross the bridge at one time. Lost in his thoughts, Robin took the bridge.

Then he noticed that a tall man had also stepped onto the bridge from the other side.

'Go back and wait till I have come over,' called out Robin to the stranger.

The stranger laughed, and called out, 'You can go back till I get across.'

Hearing this, Robin became very angry. At once, he drew an arrow from his quiver, fitted it in his bow and called out again, 'If you don't go back I'll shoot this arrow at you.'

'If you do, I'll beat you,' said the stranger. Robin Hood was surprised to hear this.

Then, the stranger said, 'Do you call it fair to attack me with bow and arrow when I only have this stick to defend myself. You are a coward.'

But Robin was not a coward. So, the next moment, he threw down his bow and arrow on the bank of the river. Then, he said, 'Wait, I shall find a stick and I shall give you a beating for your rudeness.'

The stranger laughed and said, 'I won't run away.'

Soon, Robin Hood cut himself a good, thick stick from a tree branch. In no time, he returned to the edge of the bridge with the stick. He was now smiling. You see, Robin had decided that he would cross the bridge first.

'We will fight on the bridge,' said Robin. 'Whoever first falls into the river has lost. The other shall then cross the bridge first.' 'All right,' said the stranger.

The next moment, Robin Hood and the stranger began to fight with sticks. It was very difficult to fight on a narrow bridge. The two kept swaying backwards and forwards trying to keep their balance. With every stroke the bridge bent and trembled beneath them as if it would break. Nonetheless, the two managed to give each other good blows. It soon became clear to Robin Hood and the stranger that they were both good at fighting with sticks.

Bang, smash, crack, bang, they went at each other. Their blows fell fast and thick on each other.

After some time, as Robin was winning, the stranger realized that he would soon lose. So, with all his strength, he gave a powerful blow to

Robin. The next moment, Robin fell right into the river with a splash. The next moment, he was nowhere to be seen.

The stranger had won but he was surprised to see that Robin had disappeared. He knelt down on the bridge, and cried, 'Hello, where are you?'

But no reply came. The stranger thought that Robin had drowned into the river. He was sad as he had not wanted to do that. Then, he heard Robin's voice. 'Here I am. I am all right. I am just swimming with the tide,' said Robin. The strong water of the river had taken him away from the bridge.

In a few minutes, Robin managed to reach the bridge. Holding onto the overhanging tree branches, Robin came ashore. The stranger rushed towards him.

'You are not an easy man to beat or to drown,' remarked the stranger with a laugh as Robin stood dripping.

'Well,' said Robin, laughing, 'You are a brave man and a good fighter. You have won a fair fight. Will you shake hands and be friends with me?'

'Absolutely,' said the stranger. 'It is a long time since I have met anyone who could use a stick like you.'

'I could say the same for you, said Robin Hood. 'I am Robin Hood.'

The stranger was stunned to realize that he had been fighting with the bold Robin Hood about whom he had heard so many tales.

'If you will come and live with me and my Merry Men,' went on Robin, 'I will teach you how to use bow and arrows as well as you use your good stick.'

'I should like nothing better,' said the stranger. 'My name is John Little, and I promise to serve you faithfully.'

And that is how the two had met. Since that day, Robin Hood and John Little fought together and they remained the best of friends till they grew old and died.

Complete the sentences

Recall the story you have read and complete the sentences.

1. The fast flowing river had..
2. Robin drew.. called out.
3. With each stroke.. would brake.
4. Robin fell.. be seen.
5. The stranger was surprised to realise... .... tales.
6. Robin Hood and.. .... died.

 **Pick the correct answer**

1. Robin Hood was a ....
   a. Grocer
   b. Miller
   c. Bandit

2. Robin Hood wanted to cross a...................... bridge.
   a. Wide
   b. Narrow
   c. Broad

3. A coward is a person who has no............................
   a. Kindness
   b. Courage
   c. Anger

4. To disappear is ....
   a. Go down
   b. To vanish
   c. To fall

5. The people who lived with Robin Hood were called............................
   a. Merry Men
   b. Brave Men
   c. Robin's Men

6. Robin Hood always carried his.......................... with him.
   a. His food

b. Bow and arrows

c. Flowers

Punctuation

Read the following sentences given below. Use the **capital letters**, **commas** and **full stops** in these sentences whenever it is required. Then write the sentences in the space provided.

1. the himalayas are the tallest mountains

   ....

2. shaun took a ride on his new bicycle

   ....

3. the woman had a basketful of apples oranges and mangoes

   ....

4. ray bought a sweet a pencil and a cap

   ....

5. rita had a dog called woofer

   ....

6. sam went to paris to see the eiffel tower

   ....

7. the woman bought a dozen roses

   ....

8. the birds are eating grains

   ....

Synonyms

Read the words given below in two columns. Can you match the words that have the **same** meaning?

Words	Synonyms
Bandit	Furious
Fondly	Shake
Angry	Astonishment
Surprise	Powerful
Tremble	Robber
Strong	Lovingly

Practice writing sentences

Read the words given below and use them in your sentences.

1. Pool

   ....

2. Sticks

   ....

3. Bridge

   ....

4. Match

   ....

5. Fell

   ....

6. Strong

   ....

Fun to Know

8

A warming up discussion

Which is the tallest animal you have seen?
Do you know what grasslands are?

Giraffe

Surely you have seen the tallest land animal, giraffe, perhaps in a zoo. You must have noticed that they have long legs and a very long neck. But did you know that if we stood next to a giraffe, we would be only as tall as its legs! It is also due to their long legs that giraffes can run fast. They can run as fast as 35 miles an hour.

These towering animals usually live in open grasslands in the African continent in small groups. Due to their tall height, the giraffes eat the topmost leaves of a tree. It uses its long tongue which is purplish blue to pluck leaves from the top of the trees. Giraffes are usually seen eating and these giants have to travel long distances to find food.

Have you noticed the giraffe's skin! This giant has a beautiful coat that is covered with brown spotted coat. Did you know that no two giraffes have the same pattern on their coats! Yet the giraffes can tell each other apart due to their different coats. Both male and female giraffes have two small horns on their head. Giraffes use these horns when they sometimes fight with each other playfully. But sometimes, the male giraffes, called bulls, fight each other by butting their long necks and heads. During such fights, if one animal admits defeat then the contest ends.

The giraffe's height also helps it to keep a sharp lookout for predators across the wide expanse of the grasslands. However, the giraffes need to be extra cautious when it goes to drink water. If a giraffes wants to drink water, it must spread its legs and bend down in an awkward manner. It is in this position that the predators of giraffes, the African big cats, can easily kill the giraffes. Giraffes only need to drink once every several days. It is because they get to drink most of the water they need from the leaves that they eat. Did you know that giraffes sleep for only a few minutes and they get only 30 minutes of sleep in a day!

A giraffe is always alert to the presence of its predator, the African lion. Still if it gets attacked, it uses its powerful hooves to attack its predator. Its hooves can give its predator a serious blow.

When female giraffes give birth, they do so while standing up. The baby giraffe when born falls six feet before it hits the ground. But the young remains unhurt. Interestingly, the baby giraffe can stand on its own in about half an hour or in a hour. The baby can run with its mother in about 10 hours after birth. When the small group goes to find food, one female giraffe usually remains with the children to babysit them.

So, now, don't you think it would be nice to see this incredible animal at a close range!

 **Let's remember the story**

1. Where are giraffes found?
2. Describe the skin of a giraffe.
3. How do the giraffes use their horns?
4. Why is it dangerous for a giraffe when it drinks water?
5. How can a giraffe protect itself against the African lion?
6. How much do giraffes sleep?

Idioms

A group of words which have a different meaning compared to the written/spoken words are **idioms**. Match the idioms given in Column A with their meanings in Column B.

Idioms	Meanings
A night owl	Someone or something strange
A queer fish	Very quiet
Eyes like a hawk	Very competitive
Quiet as a mouse	Someone who stays awake at night
The lion's share	Very good eyesight
The rat race	Having the biggest share

g. Circling the words

Read the passage given below and circle all the **doing words** or **verbs**.

Banks are places where people can keep their money. Most people use banks to save money. People save money in their savings accounts and they pay money from their checking accounts. Today, when a person earns money while doing a job, his or her paycheck is often electronically put into their savings or checking account. Then, he or she can pay their bills by writing checks from their checking accounts or pay online where their bills are electronically connected to their bank accounts.

Banks also give loans to people. Banks use the money that their customers keep in the bank to lend to people who want to buy new houses, cars, or to start businesses among other reasons. The bank makes money from the interest it charges when they lend money to people. In other words, people have to pay back more money than they have borrowed from the bank. This amount depends on how risky the bank thinks the borrower is and how fast the loan is paid back among other things.

Crossword

Complete the crossword with the given clues.

Across

1. The world's tallest animal
2. We drink it when thirsty
3. The king of animals
4. The continent where giraffes are found

Down

5. A large area filled with grass
6. A pointy part on animals' head

Fun to Know

A warming up discussion
What are elves?
Do you help others?

The Elves and the Shoemaker

Long ago, there lived a shoemaker with his wife in a large town. He was honest and hardworking. But no matter how hard he worked, he was unable to earn a living. As time passed, he became poorer and poorer.

One day, the shoemaker was left with just enough leather to make one pair of shoes. 'I can only make one pair of shoes with this leather,' he told his wife, sadly. 'Don't worry, something good will surely happen,' replied his wife, consoling her husband. The shoemaker cut the last pair of shoes and left the leather cutouts on his worktable before going home. The next morning, when he walked into his shop he was in for a surprise. On his worktable were kept a pair of beautiful shoes.

'What a beautiful pair of shoes!' exclaimed the shoemaker. He picked up the pair of shoes, examined them and wondered, 'Who must have made these shoes?'

Few minutes later his wife came to the shop. 'Look, someone has made such beautiful shoes out of the leather which I had cut last night,' the shoemaker said to his wife. 'Who would help us?' cried his wife who was equally surprised to see the pair of shoes.

As the shoemaker and his wife stood admiring the pair of shoes, a merchant passing by saw the shoes. He thought, 'I must buy these beautiful shoes for my wife.'

Without wasting time, the merchant offered the shoemaker two gold coins and bought the pair of shoes. The shoemaker was very happy. 'This money is enough to buy leather for two pairs of shoes,' said the shoemaker. So, he bought leather enough to make two pairs of shoes. 'Who do you think helped us?' asked the shoemaker's wife as the shoemaker cut the leather for more shoes. 'I don't know but I am grateful for the help,' replied the shoemaker.

Once again, the shoemaker left the cut leather pieces on his worktable for the night. 'I will make the shoes tomorrow,' he thought and went home.

Next morning, to his surprise, again two pairs of beautiful shoes lay on his worktable just like the previous day. 'Someone has again made the shoes,' he said. In the same manner, in no time those two pairs of shoes were also sold. And then as time passed by, it became a practice with the shoemaker to leave the leather cutouts on his worktable for the night. And each morning, beautiful pairs of shoes were on his worktable. Soon, the shoemaker became rich.

One day, the shoemaker's wife said, 'I think we should find out who has been helping us.' 'You are right! Let's hide in the shop tonight and we shall be able to find out who has been helping us,' said the shoemaker.

So, later that evening, the shoemaker and his wife hid themselves behind the curtains in the shoemaker's shop. Time passed. Then, suddenly, at the stroke of twelve, two elves hopped into the shoemaker's shop through the window. They were tiny creatures in torn clothes. They also had small hammers with them.

Immediately, they went up to his worktable, picked up the leather pieces and began to work. When the elves were done making the shoes, they hopped out of the window.

'We must thank these little elves, who have helped us in our difficult times,' said the shoemaker's wife. 'What should we do to show our gratitude to these little elves?' asked the shoemaker.

'I have an idea. I will stitch tiny trousers, shirts and socks for them while you can make tiny shoes for them,' said the shoemaker's wife. 'That is a splendid idea,' cried the shoemaker. 'Let us get to work.' And so, the next day the shoemaker and his wife were busy in making clothes and shoes for the elves.

Once they were done, the shoemaker kept the shoes and clothes on the shoemaker's worktable instead of the leather cutouts. Then once again, the couple hid themselves in the shop and waited for the elves to arrive.

Then, as always the elves arrived at midnight. But to their surprise they did not find the leather cutouts on the worktable. Instead they saw clothes and shoes, just their size kept there. Delighted, the elves put on the clothes and shoes and danced with joy. Then, slowly they made their way towards the window and hopped out.

After that day, the shoemaker did not see the elves. But as they had left they had blessed the shoemaker. The shoemaker always prospered for now he knew how to make lovely shoes.

 **Let's remember the story**

1. What happened when the shoemaker left the leather cutouts in his shop?
2. How much money did he receive for the pair of shoes?
3. Who had been helping the shoemaker?
4. How did the shoemaker thank the elves?
5. Why do you think the shoemaker was poor?
6. What happened when the elves saw the shoes and clothes?

Think and fill

Read the following sentences. Fill in the blanks using the correct articles, **a**, **an**, and **the**.

1. ....few children were playing in........ park.

2. I made........... lemonade.

3. I saw............ moon each night.

4. .... capital of Spain is Madrid.

5. Have you got............ pencil?

6. Martha had............ orange for lunch.

Prefix and suffix

Given below are a few **prefix** and **suffix** along with a number of words. Let us see if you remember how to use them to make new words.

un-	in-	-ness	-ly

real	even	told	kind	spire	action
field	aware	bald	blind	dark	apt
awful	bad	bright			

....

....

....

....

Practice writing sentences

Read the words given below and use them in your sentences.

1. Honest

   ....

2. Admire

   ....

3. Surprise

   ....

4. Tiny

   ....

5. Difficult

   ....

6. Dance

   ....

Fun to Know

10

A warming up discussion
Have you flown in an airplane?
Do you know what a helicopter is?

Helicopter

You must have seen helicopters. But have you ever thought about when they were first made and how they fly! The idea of a machine that you can fly in the sky was first thought of hundreds of years ago. But it was Italian inventor Leonardo Da Vinci, during the 1500s, who first put the idea of a flying machine into a drawing. Experts say that this drawing inspired the modern day helicopter. This drawing is named Ornithopter. Years passed by. Then, in 1784, French inventor Launoy and Bienvenue made a toy with a rotary-wing that could lift and fly around and it thus proved the principle of helicopter flight.

Did you know that helicopter moves when the air above its rotors moves! This moving air helps the helicopter to lift itself from the ground! As the idea of flying become popular, the designs for a flying machine were developed. It was in 1863 that French writer Ponton D'Amecourt coined the term 'helicopter' from the two words 'helico' which means spiral and 'pter' meaning wings.

In 1907, Paul Cornu invented the first piloted helicopter but his model wasn't successful. But this small failure did not stop the others. There were many others who had developed workable designs for a helicopter.

But it was Igor Sikorsky who first made a successful model of a helicopter. It was his design of the helicopter upon which further helicopter designs were made. He is thus called the father of helicopters. One of aviation's greatest designers, Igor Sikorsky began working on the helicopters as early as 1910. By 1940, he had modified his designs so much and was so successful that his design of VS-300 became the model for all modern single-rotor helicopters. He also designed and built the first military helicopter, XR-4.

Igor Sikorsky's helicopters were the first helicopters that had the control to fly safely forwards, backwards, sideways and up and down. Do you know that a helicopter can hover in the sky without moving for sometime! In 1958, Igor Sikorsky's rotorcraft company was also successful in making a helicopter that could land and takeoff even from water. This helicopter could even float on water.

In 1944, American inventor Stanley Hiller Jr. made the first helicopter with very stiff all metal rotor blades. These stiff rotor blades allowed the helicopters to fly at much higher speeds. And since that day, many more advancements have been made in the field of helicopters. Do you know that helicopters are also called 'chopper' or a 'helo'?

Over the years, helicopters have been put to many uses. It is because helicopter can go places where airplanes cannot go. Helicopters are used to rescue people who are stuck on mountains, in oceans and during storms. It is also used by the police. Helicopters are used to take ill persons to the hospital, to know the traffic of a city, to send supplies to those in need, to spray water when there is a fire in a house or a building or in the forest and also to take people from one place to another quickly. So, when are you up for a helicopter ride?

Complete the sentences

Recall what you have read about helicopters and complete the sentences.

1. Leonardo da Vinci put.. drawing.

2. Helicopters move.. moves.

3. Igor Sikorsky first.. ....

4. Helicopters can fly.. and down.

5. Stiff rotor blades allow... speeds.

6. Helicopters are used to rescue ....

Antonyms

Read the words given below in two columns. Can you match the words that have the **opposite** meaning?

Words	Antonyms
Gentle	Sink
Float	There
Inside	Dark
Great	Rough
Light	Outside
Here	Tiny

Pick the odd one out

Read the words given below. Circle the word that do not belong to the group.

1. Air Transport: airplane, helicopter, glider, bicycle

2. Water Transport: boat, motorcycle, ship, steamer

3. Land Transport: car, bus, raft, train

4. Space Transport: rocket, airplane, space shuttle

5. Cable Transport: trams, cycle, elevators, ski lift

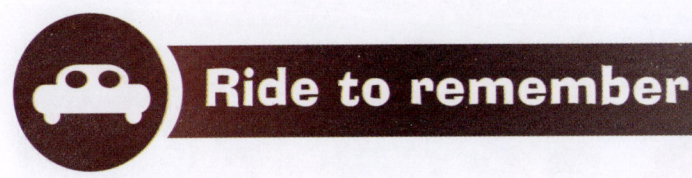

Ride to remember

You must have a bicycle which you ride or perhaps you must have taken a ride on a car, bus or a train. Tell us about a particular ride on a vehicle that you enjoyed the most.

Chopper Savvy!

Helicopters fly differently from airplanes. They need a small space to land and to take off. Wouldn't it be nice to know more about helicopters and how they work with the help of your teacher!

Fun to Know

A warming up discussion
How many friends do you have?
How much time do you spend with your friends everyday?

Friends
Abbie Farwell Brown

How good to lie a little while
And look up through the tree!
The Sky is like a kind big smile
Bent sweetly over me.

The Sunshine flickers through the lace
Of leaves above my head,
And kisses me upon the face
Like Mother, before bed.

The Wind comes stealing o'er the grass
To whisper pretty things;
And though I cannot see him pass,
I feel his careful wings.

So many gentle Friends are near
Whom one can scarcely see,
A child should never feel a fear,
Wherever he may be.

✓ Complete the sentences

Now that you have read the poem, let us complete the sentences.

1. Sky is like a.. over me.

2. And kisses me.. before bed.

3. The wind over grass whispers..

4. So many gentle.. scarcely see.

5. ....him pass.. wings.

6. ....flickers.. my head.

In the park!

You are in the park. You are relaxing lying under a tree. It is early morning. Write about all that you see around you. Can you see any of the invisible friends that are talked about in the poem?

....
....
....
....
....

Punctuation

Read the following sentences given below. Use the **capital letters**, **commas** and **full stops** in these sentences whenever it is required. Then write the sentences in the space provided.

1. the sun is shining in the sky
   ....

2. a soft breeze is blowing
   ....

3. nancy is picking up flowers
   ....

4. the cat is climbing a tree
   ....

5. jim dan and tony are running on the grass
   ....

6. girls and boys are learning karate
   ....

7. leaves are falling on the ground
   ....

8. the dog is running after the butterflies
   ....

Synonyms

Read the words given below in two columns. Can you match the words that have the **same** meaning?

Words	Synonyms
Sweet	Fright
Joy	Cautious
Careful	Pleasing
Fear	Barely
Scarcely	Cheerful
Happy	Delight

Fun to Know

12 **A warming up discussion**
Who is Harry Potter?
Do you know who had thought of creating Harry Potter?

J. K. Rowling

Joanne Kathleen Rowling, also famous as J.K Rowling was born on July 31, 1965, in Chipping Sodbury, near Bristol, England. She was the daughter of Peter James Rowling and Anne Volant. While Rowling was four years old, his family moved to Winterbourne. Here she met a brother and sister whose last name was Potter. When she was nine years old, her family moved again. In school, Rowling worked hard in her studies but she never had much flair for sports. Later, at 18 years of age, Rowling attended the University of Exeter where she studied French.

After she had completed her college, she did a number of jobs. Then in 1990, during a train journey, Rowling came up with the concept of Harry Potter. She says that the idea "simply fell into my mind." But soon due to her mother's death and in order to make herself come out of her sorrow, Rowling accepted a job offer to teach English in Portugal. It was also here that she got married to a Portuguese journalist Jorge Arantes. They had one daughter. But sadly, the marriage did not last for long.

So, Rowling moved to Edinburgh to live with her sister Di. Life was difficult to raise a child as a single mother, so Rowling fell back on the idea that had occurred to her during the train ride. In 1995, she finished typing out 'Harry Potter and the Philosopher's Stone' and sent it out to various literary agents. A reader called Bryony Evans, at Christopher Little literary agents, at once recognised the potential of her work. And so, the firm sent the book to at least twelve publishers. After a year long wait, Rowling had found a publisher in Bloomsbury. There is a publishing legend that the decision to publish the book owes much to Alice Newton, the eight-year-old daughter of Bloomsbury's chairman!

And so, Rowling's first book *Harry Potter and the Sorcerer's Stone* was published in June 1997, with an initial print run of one thousand copies, 500 of which were sold to libraries. The book, and its subsequent series, chronicled the life of Harry Potter, a young wizard, and his multi-coloured band at the Hogwarts School of Witchcraft and Wizardry. As her books gained more exposure, Rowling's talent and ability as a children's writer became more established.

Rowling became an international literary sensation in 1999, when the first three installments of her Harry Potter books came on the top three slots of *The New York Times* best-seller list. When the fourth volume in the series was published in 2000, *Harry Potter and the Goblet of Fire*, it became the fastest-selling book in history! In 1998, one short year after her first book had seen print, she sold the film rights for her first two books to Warner Brothers which made her a millionaire overnight. And since then there has been no looking back.

In December 2001, Rowling married Neil Michael Murray, an anaesthetist, in a private ceremony at her home in Aberfeldy, Scotland. J.K. Rowling is the most celebrated and recognized children's writer today.

Let's remember the story

1. Whom had Rowling met in Winterbourne?
2. How does she describe the idea about writing 'Harry Potter'?
3. Her first book was sent to many publishers. How many?
4. What is the Harry Potter series about?
5. What was the original name of Harry Potter and the Sorcerer's stone?
6. Which is the fastest selling book in history?

Become a writer!

Imagine, think and complete the story given below.

It was a beautiful day. It was Max's birthday. He was excited about the present he would get. Mom and dad opened the door to his room..............

....

....

....

....

....

....

....

....

Find friends

You are familiar with similar sounding words called **rhyming words**. Read the words in Column A aloud and write a similar sounding word in front of them in Column B.

Column A	Column B
Move	Fighter
Flair	Blot
Sorrow	Germ
Firm	Prove
Writer	Borrow
Slot	Chair

Antonyms

Read the words given below in the first column. Can you write the words that are the **opposite** of the given word?

Words	Antonyms
Many	
Odd	
Neat	
Strong	
Sorrow	
Take	

Fun to Know

A warming up discussion
What wish would you ask of a genie?
What would you do if it is granted?

King Midas' Touch

Characters:

Narrator   King Midas   King's daughter   God Dionysus

Script

Narrator: Long, long ago there lived a king called Midas. He was a kind king and was loved by his people. But the king had a weakness for gold. One day, he helped God Dionysus.

God Dionysus: Midas, you have greatly pleased me. So, I shall give you one boon.

King Midas: God Dionysus, I am happy that I have been able to help you. I want nothing else.

God Dionysus: That may be so. But I have promised you a boon.

King Midas: If you so like, God Dionysus then grant me the boon that whatever I touch turns into gold.

God Dionysus: Midas, have you thought about what you are asking? You might get into trouble.

King Midas: My Lord that is the boon I want.

Narrator: When God Dionysus saw that Midas had decided, he said...

God Dionysus: Then, so be it.

Narrator: Saying so, God Dionysus disappeared in a flash of light. Now, King Midas decided to test the boon that he had been given. So, he rushed to his palace garden. There, he touched a flower and it turned into gold.

He touched a piece of rock and it turned into gold too!

King Midas: Ah! How wonderful! Everything that I touch turns into gold. My kingdom shall be the richest.

Narrator: Later, the king sat down to dine. But the moment, he touched the food....

King Midas: My food has turned to gold too. What shall I eat now! What shall I drink!

Narrator: King Midas was troubled. He realised now why God Dionysus had asked him to reconsider his request. Just then, Midas's daughter came to meet him. She looked sad.

King Midas: What is the matter, my dear? Why are you so sad?

King's daughter: Father, I had a.....

Narrator: But she could not complete her sentence for King Midas had touched her daughter's hand to console her and the next instant she too had turned to gold.

King Midas: What have I done? My beloved daughter too has been turned to gold! What will I do now?

Narrator: Then, lamenting King Midas prayed to God Dionysus. The god appeared before him.

King Midas: Please, take back the boon that you had granted me.

God Dionysus: I had warned you Midas. But you did not listen to me. I also cannot take back the boon that I had given you.

King Midas: But there must be a way, My Lord.

God Dionysus: Midas, then you must go to River Pactolus and take a bath in its waters and only then will your boon be washed away.

King Midas: Thank you, My Lord. I am grateful to you.

Narrator: Then, King Midas without wasting another moment rushed to River Pactolus and took a bath in the waters of the river. When he stepped out, he touched a tree but it remained as it was. Soon, he returned to his palace and saw his daughter running towards him. He was overjoyed to see his daughter.

King Midas: Oh! I am so grateful. In Future, I shall think before I shall ask for any boons.

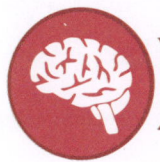 ## Let's remember the story

1. What was the weakness of King Midas?
2. What did God Dionysus want to give King Midas?
3. What boon did King Midas ask for?
4. Why was King Midas unable to eat his food?
5. Why did King Midas ask God Dionysus to take back his boon?
6. How did King Midas get rid of his boon?

 ## Think and fill

Read the following sentences. Fill in the blanks using the correct articles, **a**, **an**, and **the**.

1. ....Nile is the longest river in......... world.
2. We saw.......... elephant in........... Zoo.
3. ....sparrow is sitting on my window sill.
4. He is...... tallest boy in my class.
5. ...... girl fell into..... puddle.

6. .... police caught...... thief.

7. Did you get........ umbrella?

8. Have you received....... letter?

 **Idioms**

A group of words which have a different meaning compared to the written/spoken words are **idioms**. Match the idioms given in Column A with their meanings in Column B.

Idioms	Meanings
A piece of cake	Something unusual
Against the clock	Starting all over again
Apple of my eye	Short on time
Back to square one	To eat
A blue moon	Someone liked more above others
Chow Down	An easy task

Plan a Skit!

The children can perform a short skit on the story 'Emperor's new clothes'. The teacher can write the script and a few children can enact the story. The teacher can undertake a question answer session based on the skit when it is over.

Fun to Know

A warming up discussion

Have you been home alone?
- What did you do then?

The Wolf and the Seven Young Kids

Once upon a time there was an old goat that had seven little kids. One day she wanted to go into the woods to get some food. So she called all seven kids to her and said, 'Children, I am going into the woods. Do not open the door for anyone. The clever wolf may come, if he gets in, he will eat up all of you. You will be able to recognize him by his rough voice and his black feet.' The kids said, 'Mother dear, we will remember all you said and we will take care of ourselves.'

With her mind at ease, the goat went to the woods. It was not long before someone knocked at the door and called out, 'Open the door, children, your mother is back.'

But the little kids knew from the rough voice that it was the wolf.

'We will not open the door,' they cried out. 'You are not our mother. She has a soft and gentle voice, but your voice is rough. You are the wolf.'

So the wolf went to a shopkeeper and bought himself a large piece of chalk, which he ate, making his voice soft. Then he came back and knocked at the door, calling out, 'Open the door, children. Your mother is back.'

But as the wolf stood at the door, he laid one of his black paws on the window by the door. The children saw his paw and cried out, 'We will not open the door. Our mother does not have a black foot like you. You are the wolf.'

The wolf was disappointed. This time he ran to a baker and said, 'I have sprained my foot. Rub some dough on it for me.' When it was done, the wolf ran to the miller and said, 'Sprinkle some white flour on my foot for me.'

The miller said, 'I won't do it. You are going to trick someone.' 'If you will not do it, I will eat you,' said the wolf angrily. The frightened miller did as he was told.

Then once again, the wolf knocked on the door and said, 'Open the door for me, children. Your dear mother has come home.'

'Show us your paw so we may know that you are our mother,' cried the kids.

Without hesitation, the wolf placed his paw on the window. 'It is mother!' cried the kids happily and opened the door. But who came in? It was the wolf! The kids were frightened and ran around the house to hide themselves. One jumped under the table, the second into the bed, the third into the stove, the fourth into the kitchen, the fifth inside the cupboard, the sixth under the washbasin and the seventh into the clock case. But in no time, the wolf found them all and swallowed them. Then he went out of the house and into the meadow where he fell asleep under a shady tree. He had however been unable to find the youngest kid, the one who had hid in the clock case.

Soon the mother goat returned home. Oh, what a sight she saw there. The door stood wide open. Table, chairs, and benches were tipped over. Everything in the house was scattered or broken. And her kids were nowhere to be found. She called her kids but no one answered. It was then that a soft voice cried out, 'Mother dear, I am hiding in the clock case.' Hurriedly, the mother goat took out her youngest kid and learnt how the wolf had eaten her kids. How sad she was! But she was also grateful that one of her kids had survived.

Finally, in her grief, she went towards the meadow with her youngest kid. In the meadow, they saw the wolf snoring loudly under a shady tree. It was then that she noticed something moving inside the wolf's belly.

'Good gracious,' she thought. 'Is it possible that my poor children can still be alive in his belly?' At once, the mother goat sent the youngest kid home to fetch scissors and a needle and thread. When everything was brought, she cut open the wolf's belly. She had scarcely done so when one of her kid's head popped out. And then one after the other her six kids hopped out of the wolf's belly. How happy they all were to see each other! You see, the wolf had swallowed them all in his greed instead of eating them. So, they were all alive.

Then, the mother goat said, 'Quickly, bring some big stones to fill the wolf's belly.' The seven kids in a jiffy did so. Mother Goat then put the stones in the wolf's belly and sewed it up using needle and thread. Then, she and her kids went back home. And all this while, the wolf felt nothing.

After some time, the wolf woke up. He felt thirsty. But when he woke up he felt that his belly was too heavy. As he went towards the well, he felt the stones knocking against each other in his belly. 'With this rumbling in my stomach, I feel as if the kids were stones,' said the wolf. But somehow he managed to reach the well. But no sooner had he leaned over the well to drink water that the heavy stones pulled him into the well and the wolf drowned.

The seven kids had seen the wolf as he drowned and jumped for joy crying, 'The Wolf is dead!' And never again any wolf troubled them again.

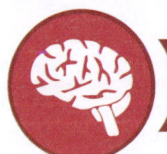 **Let's remember the story**

1. What did the mother goat warn her kids about?
2. How did the kids recognize that it was the wolf the first time he came?
3. What did the wolf do to make his paw white?
4. Where did the seventh kid hid himself?
5. What did the mother goat think seeing the wolf's belly moving?

6. What did the mother goat and her kids fill in the wolf's belly?

Punctuation

Read the following sentences given below. Use the **capital letters**, **commas** and **full stops** in these sentences whenever it is required. Then write the sentences in the space provided.

1. john plays football well

   ....

2. kangaroos only live in australia

   ....

3. helicopters can also land on buildings

   ....

4. mother bought me a dress ribbons and shoes

   ....

5. father bought a new car

   ....

6. france is a country in europe

   ....

7. the sunflowers turn towards the sun

   ....

8. he bought brushes colours and sheets to paint

   ....

Practice writing sentences

Read the words given below and use them in your sentences.

1. Clever

   ....

   ....

2. Rough

   ....

   ....

3. Trick

   ....

   ....

4. Open

   ....

   ....

5. Jump

   ....

   ....

5. Shady

   ....

   ....

Words and their meanings

Read the words given below. With the help of a dictionary find out the meanings of the given words and write the meanings in the space provided.

Word	Meaning
Recognize	
Remember	
Frighten	
Scatter	
Trouble	
Drown	

Fun to Know

15 A warming up discussion

Do you know about Halloween?
What happens during Halloween?

Halloween

Halloween is a festival that is celebrated with great enthusiasm in many parts of the world. You must have heard about it or seen people especially children dressed up as ghosts, witches and goblins. It must have looked like fun. Compared to what people think today, the Halloween festival had started many hundred of years ago. But the reasons and the traditions that were attached with this festival have changed with time.

Halloween, one of the oldest festivals, was originally a Celtic festival. Way back then this festival was called Samhain. It was celebrated to mark the end of the harvesting season and also to mark the beginning of a new year. This New Year began on November 1. The Celtics also believed that ghosts and spirits roamed the earth at this time. So, in order to protect themselves they lit bonfires as protection.

Later, when the Romans took over the Celtic lands, they adapted the Celtic festival of Samhain, to honour their own deities. One of these deities was Pomona. She was the goddess of fruit and trees and was represented by an apple. This may be why we bob for apples at Halloween parties today! Apple bobbing is a game played on the day of Halloween. In it apples are put in a large container which is filled with water. Those who play the game must pick up the apples with their teeth as the float in the water. Using your hands is not allowed. Would you like to play Apple Bobbing?

Later, when Christianity took over, the festival of Samhain went through another change. The Roman Catholic Church adapted this day as All Saints', or All Hallows' Day, to honour those saints who did not have a specific feast day to honour them. The mass that took place on this day was called 'Allhallowmas.' With time, the All Hallows Day got shortened to Halloween.

During this day, the tradition of trick-or-treating was also started along with All Souls' Day parades in England. During the festivities, the villagers gave poor people 'soul cakes' in return for the prayers for their dead relatives. As the festival reached America, it again underwent a change.

By now, the festival of Halloween was no longer religious. It had become a holiday where children began to go trick-or-treating in their neighbourhoods. Now, people and especially children wore various costumes for one night. It also became an inexpensive way for people to celebrate together. Another reason to wear scary costumes is to scare the spirits that roam the world on Allhallowseve. So, the children began dressing up as witches, ghosts, vampires and other scary creatures and went trick-or-treating.

Trick-or-treating is an activity for children, also a main tradition, on or around Halloween in which they proceed from house to house in costumes, asking for treats such as confectionery with the question, 'Trick or Treat?' The trick part is a threat to play a trick on the person or his property if no treat is given.

Along with trick-or-treating, bonfires, costume parties, visiting 'haunted houses' and carving jack-o-lanterns also became popular with people. Other countries have their own celebrations at this time but with different meanings. In Mexico, people celebrate El Dia de los Muertos which means the Day of the Dead. This is a time to honor and celebrate the dead.

So, when are you going to wear a costume and go trick-or-treating!

 **Complete the sentences**

You have read the chapter now let us complete the sentences.

1. Halloween was..
2. The Celtics believed..
   .... earth.
3. Pamona was the goddess..
   .... She was represented...
4. ....shortened to
   ....
5. Children dress as..
   on this day.

6. ....a children's activity.

Festival maze

Find the given words in the maze below.

Halloween ghosts treat saints lantern celebrate Celtic harvest

G	E	W	L	A	N	T	E	R	N
H	H	A	L	L	O	W	E	E	N
O	A	U	R	C	E	L	T	I	C
S	T	R	O	T	I	L	I	A	L
T	N	W	V	R	H	U	R	L	P
S	C	E	L	E	B	R	A	T	E
S	T	N	I	A	S	H	T	E	N
R	O	C	T	T	S	T	K	O	E

g) Circling the words

Read the passage given below and circle all the **describing words** or **adjectives**.

Sue was a little girl. She was kind and intelligent. But she was lonely. Sue had no friends near their new home. Her mother saw that her dear daughter was unhappy. She then had an idea.

One day, mother went to a pet store. When she returned she had a small basket with her. The basket was covered with a black cloth. Mother and father went to Sue's lovely room. They placed the basket near her low table. Sue came curiously towards the basket. Slowly, she picked up the cloth. There was an adorable, brown puppy inside the basket! How happy Sue was! Each day, Sue played with the puppy called biscuit in the beautiful garden before their house. When the children saw the puppy, they too came to play with Sue. Sue soon made new friends. She was never alone again.

Think and fill

Read the following sentences. Fill in the blanks using the correct articles, **a**, **an**, and **the**.

1. ....Earth is called a blue planet.

2. Girls are skipping in........... park.

3. ....rainbow forms after it rains.

4. Rhinoceros has..... horn on his head.

5. ....old woman lives in that house.

6. ....hen has laid........... egg.

7. Jack climbed..... beanstalk.

8. Mother bought........... dozen apples.

Your favourite festival!

Let us know what festival do you like the most. Why is this festival your favourite? What do you do on your favourite festival? Write a few lines on the space given below.

....

....

....

....

....
....
....
....
....
....

Fun to Know

16 **A warming up discussion**
What is a fieldmouse?
Where does it live?

The Fieldmouse
by Cecil Frances Alexander

Where the acorn tumbles down,
Where the ash tree sheds its berry,
With your fur so soft and brown,
With your eye so round and merry,
Scarcely moving the long grass,
Fieldmouse, I can see you pass.

Little thing, in what dark den,
Lie you all the winter sleeping?
Till warm weather comes again,
Then once more I see you peeping
Round about the tall tree roots,
Nibbling at their fallen fruits.

Fieldmouse, fieldmouse, do not go,
Where the farmer stacks his treasure,
Find the nut that falls below,
Eat the acorn at your pleasure,
But you must not steal the grain
He has stacked with so much pain.

Let's remember the story

1. Where does the narrator see the fieldmouse?
2. How does he describe the fieldmouse?
3. Where does he lie during the winter?
4. Where is the fieldmouse seen during the summer?
5. What does the narrator advice the fieldmouse?
6. What has the farmer 'stacked with so much pain'?

Antonyms

Read the words given below in two columns. Can you match the words that have **opposite** meaning?

Words	Antonyms
Melt	Quiet
Neat	Under
Noisy	Messy
Old	Freeze
Over	Safe
Dangerous	Young

Words and their meanings

Read the words given below. With the help of a dictionary find out the meanings of the given words and write the meanings in the space provided.

Words	Meanings
Scarce	
Nibble	
Treasure	
Steal	
Stack	
Tumble	

Greenhouse here I come!

The teacher can take the students to a greenhouse. The children will observe the plants that grow in the greenhouse. They will also get to learn how a farmer grows crops in a field. The children can write about what they have learnt in a few lines.

Fun to Know

17

A warming up discussion

What is a waterfall?
Where does all that water come from?

Victoria Falls

Which is the longest waterfall you have seen? Have you ever heard of a waterfall that is 1.7 kilometres wide! Well, the Victoria Falls are the widest waterfalls in the world. They are 1.7 kilometres long. These amazing waterfalls are located in Southern Africa on the Zambezi River between the countries of Zambia and Zimbabwe. This waterfall is called Modi-oa-Tunya by the local people which means 'the smoke that thunders.' The place where this waterfall falls makes a spectacular view. Scottish explorer and missionary David Livingstone was the first European who had seen the waterfalls. It was he who had named the waterfalls as Victoria Falls after Queen Victoria.

The Victoria Falls is not the highest waterfall in the world, it is however the largest. When one looks at the Victoria Falls, it seems as if a huge curtain of water is flowing. This wonder of Africa is among the seven natural wonders of the world. Did you know that the Victoria Falls lies exactly halfway down the Zambezi River!

Victoria Falls is roughly twice the height of North America's famous Niagara Falls. It is also two times the width of the Horseshoe Falls. This waterfall is also known for three things—spray, mist and rainbow. As this immense sheet of water falls down with a thundering sound, the water gets sprayed to a height of over 400 m. Sometimes, during the flood season, the volume of water increases, the spray can rise up to a height of 800 m. To someone standing near the waterfall, it seems as if it is raining. Did you know that this spray can be seen from a distance of upto 50 kilometres! Interestingly, due to the spray, the forest around the waterfall gets rain all the time.

The Victoria Falls are also covered in mist as the water falls down on the Basalt rocks with great speed. Usually, the rocks in the gorge where the water falls can be seen. But during the rainy season, it is impossible to see the bottom of the waterfalls due to the constant thick mist. Rainbows are among the other features of Victoria Falls. Due to the spray and the mist, rainbows are frequently seen. Did you know that moonbows also form over Victoria Falls on the night of the full moon? The colours of the moonbow are the same as are seen in a rainbow.

When David Livingstone had first seen the Victoria Falls, he had said, '...it (Victoria Falls) has never been seen before by European eyes, but scenes so wonderful must have been gazed upon by angels in their flight.' Today an island near the waterfalls is named Livingstone Island in honour of the Scottish explorer.

✓ Complete the sentences

You have read the chapter now complete the sentences.

1. Victoria Falls are in.. on the...
2. In local language they are called...
3. Scottish explorer and missionary... European to see them.
4. He named the... in honour of..
5. Victoria Falls are known for..................... These three things are..
6. Along with rainbows... on full moon nights.

⇄ Prefix and suffix

Given below are a few **prefix** and **suffix** along with a number of words. Let us see if you remember how to use them to make new words.

un-	de-	-able	-y
able   arm   feat   favour   edge   glass
do   clear code   compose control class
coy   port   comfort luck

....	....	....	....
....	....	....	....
....	....	....	....
....	....	....	....

g) Circling the words

Read the passage given below and circle all the **doing words** or **verbs**.

It was a breezy day. The tree leaves were rustling due to the breeze. The sun too was not shining brightly. It was getting difficult to stand due to the strong breeze. The people in the park were looking towards the sky. Children were busy running, skipping and playing their games. Soon dark clouds covered the sky.

Then the clouds thundered. The children stopped their playing. Then pit pat, pit pat, big raindrops started falling. The children cried filled with joy. The people ran here and there looking for shelter. Soon, the raindrops started falling heavily. The children too ran towards their homes. The lights in the park were now turned on as it had become dark. Today, it was raining after many days. The rainy season had come.

Discover Waterfalls

Make a list of famous waterfalls, learn their names and spellings and see where they are. The teacher can help you in learning about the famous waterfalls of the world.

Fun to Know

A warming up discussion

Have you seen a ship?

If you were a sailor, by what name would you like to be called? The name has to make others fear you.

Sindbad the Sailor

Long ago, in the times of Caliph Haroun-al-Raschid, there lived in Baghdad a famous sailor called Sindbad. He had had many voyages across the world and had become rich. He also liked to recall his adventures for his friends. Today, was another such day, when he had called his friends on a feast and on their request, he began telling them about another of his amazing voyage across the sea.

'After my first voyage, I had decided to spend my days in Baghdad. But very soon I grew tired of such an idle life and longed to go to the sea,' began Sindbad. 'So, I bought goods to sell and began my second voyage with some known merchants. We made great profit as we went to different islands selling our goods. One day, we landed on an island covered with fruit trees and springs.

While my companions wandered here and there gathering fruits, I fell asleep in a shady place. When I opened my eyes I realised to my horror that I was alone on the island and the ship was long gone! I lamented on my fate. At last, I climbed a tall tree and looked around to see where I was.

Suddenly, at a distance I saw a huge dazzling white object. I could not make out what it was. So, I hastily collected whatever things I had with me and set off towards the strange white object. As I drew nearer, I saw that it was a white oval shaped object of immense size and height. When I touched it, I found it marvellously smooth. I tried to climb it but it was an impossible task; neither was there any opening in it of any sort.

By this time sunset was near. But suddenly, it grew dark. Then, as I watched, a bird of extraordinary size began hovering over the white object. It was a Roc, a huge bird about whom sailors often talk about. As I watched, the bird came down further until it touched the white object which was its egg!

The Roc settled down upon the egg and covered it with its wings to keep it warm. Suddenly, I knew how to get out of this island. I carefully crept near the bird, bound my turban around its leg and tied myself to the Roc's leg with the help of my turban. Soon tired, I fell asleep. Suddenly, rushing wind woke me up. It was morning and I was airborne. I was happy to be going away from the island.

A little later, the Roc came down swiftly. When it had settled on the ground, I hastily unbound my turban from its leg and freed myself. Soon after, the bird flew away with a huge snake in its beak. As I looked around, I found myself in a deep and narrow valley which was surrounded by

steep mountains. And to my great surprise, this valley was strewn with diamonds of astonishing sizes! I had not seen their like anywhere. Also, I noticed a strange hissing sound all over the valley. I could not place it correctly until I saw a huge snake moving in a hole. This valley was also home to many enormous snakes! I was frightened but they came out only at night.

All day long, I tried to find a way out of the valley. But I saw none. So, when it grew dark, I crept into a little cave I had found and blocked the entrance with a stone. I ate the little food that remained with me from the ship and lay down to sleep. But the horrible hissing all around kept me awake. Next morning, I stepped out of the cave trembling and sat down on a rock.

Suddenly something heavy fell on the ground behind me. As I turned astonished, I saw a huge piece of meat! As I stared at it, several more pieces rolled over the cliffs at different places.

'Where are these meat pieces coming from?' I wondered.

And I remembered the stories I had heard from many sailors. They had talked of a famous diamond valley and today I was in that valley. I remembered that in order to get the diamonds, the merchants threw great lumps of meat into the valley. The diamonds got stuck to these lumps of meat. These lumps of meat were then picked up by the eagles who carried them to their nests. When the eagles reached their nest, the merchants scared away the birds with shouts and cries. The moment the eagles were gone, the merchants climbed up to the nests and collected the diamonds. Remembering this, gave me an idea to escape. Quickly, I picked up all the largest diamonds I could find and put them in my bag. Then using my turban, I tied myself to a large piece of meat. Moments later, a large eagle seized the piece of meat to which I was tied and soared into the air. Minutes later, I was dropped in its nest.

No sooner was I dropped in the nest with the meat that the merchants started making a great noise and scared the eagles away from their nest. But when the merchants saw me they were disappointed. Others,

however, were surprised to see me. 'Oh! You have cost us our profit. Now we would have to drop the lumps of meat again,' said a merchant.

'I am sure friends, if you would know about my sufferings, you would show more kindness towards me,' said I. 'And as for diamonds, I have plenty! We can all distribute them among ourselves.'

Hearing this, the merchants agreed to listen to my story. We all climbed down the tree and the merchants took me to their camp. There when they heard my story, they admired the way by which I had escaped the diamond valley. I then showed them the diamonds I had collected. When they saw the diamonds, the merchants were awestruck. The diamonds were large and dazzling!

'We have never seen diamonds this huge! They are beautiful and even one diamond is enough to make us all extremely rich overnight,' they said.

I learnt that the merchants were bound for Baghdad, so I accompanied them. As we had expected, the diamonds fetched us a lot of money and nobody was complaining. Meanwhile, I was happy to be with my family once again. Again, I thought of leading a peaceful and contented life with my family. But it was only a matter of few months before I wanted to go on a voyage again. And so, forgetting all the perils I had faced in my earlier voyages, I prepared again to sail. But that is another story to tell. 'For now, my friends, enjoy this feast,' said Sindbad and began entertaining his guests.

 ## Let's remember the story

1. Who was Sindbad? Why was he famous?
2. What did Sindbad see on the island?
3. How did he escape from the island?
4. What did Sindbad see in the valley? Why was he afraid?
5. How did he land up in the nest of an eagle?
6. Why were the merchants angry seeing Sindbad?

 ## Relating objects

Read the following sentences given below. Use the **capital letters**, **commas** and **full stops** in these sentences whenever it is required. Then, write the sentences in the space provided.

1. the street dogs are barking

   ....

2. mr keith has lost his watch

   ....

3. the man has two fish a crab and a lobster in his bucket

   ....

4. lily bought a scarf a hat and a coat

5. pacific ocean is the largest ocean in the world

....

6. the postman brought letters for the smiths

....

7. the kids are dancing in the garage

....

8. the kids are making a sandwich

....

 ## Prepositions

Fill in the blanks using the prepositions given below.

by	in	at	on	up	for	over	between

1. He is waiting..................... the bus.
2. The cat is leaping..................... the fence.
3. Suzy is sitting.................... her parents.
4. You can look up for the word........ the dictionary.
5. The story was written......... the old gentleman.
6. Someone is knocking........ the door.
7. They went......... the hill.
8. She was looking....... that dress.

Crossword

Complete the crossword using the clues.

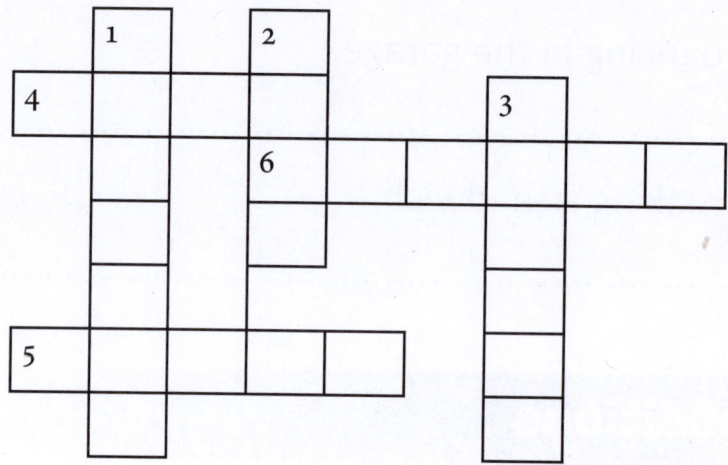

Down

1. Shiny stones Sindbad found in the valley
2. A large boat
3. Someone who sails in a ship

Across

4. Someone who has lots of money
5. It moves on the ground and has no legs
6. A land surrounded with water on all sides

Watch the movie **'Pirates of the Caribbean: The Curse of the Black Pearl'**! If it can be arranged, the movie can be seen using a projector in school.